DISCUSSION PAPER 67

I0026759

CRITICAL FACTORS IN THE HORN OF AFRICA'S RAGING CONFLICTS

KIDANE MENGISTEAB

NORDISKA AFRIKAINSTITUTET, UPPSALA 2011

Indexing terms:
Horn of Africa
Regional conflicts
Historical analysis
Social implications
Economic implications
International relations
Conflict management
Peace research

Language checking: Peter Colenbrander

ISSN 1104-8417

ISBN 978-91-7106-707-4

© The author and Nordiska Afrikainstitutet 2011

Production: Byrå4

Print on demand, Lightning Source UK Ltd.

Contents

Foreword

This Discussion Paper provides a broad overview of the causes, dynamics and ramifications of violent conflicts in the Horn of Africa, widely regarded as the most conflict-affected sub-region in Africa. It also proffers reasons as to why the conflicts will persist for some time. An in-depth analysis of the conflicts in Somalia, Ethiopia, Sudan and Uganda is undertaken. These conflicts are categorised as inter-state, intra-state and communal, and the core and contextual factors driving them are critically discussed. The conflicts are then critically examined from regional, national and local perspectives, providing both a rich historical background and an analytical framework for understanding the connections between and specificities of the complex conflicts ravaging the region. Emphasis is placed on the roots of the conflict, their interconnectedness and their impact on the region and beyond, including regional development. The paper then provides insights into the failings of the postcolonial states and how fragmentation of institutional systems fed the regional dynamics of violent conflict. Other dimensions explored include the crises of regional governance and external intervention by global powers intent on pursuing their strategic and economic interests in this region. Some attention is then paid to how the institutional and socioeconomic challenges are further complicated by environmental degradation, displacement and the refugee problem. The foregoing helps explain why none of the eight countries of the Greater Horn area is completely free of conflict and its consequences and opens up the discussion about what is needed to brighten the prospects for long-term peace. Central to the recommendations to this end is the need to address the core and contextual challenges of diversity management, nation-building, democratisation and institutional reform at all levels. The author also identifies areas for further research as a first step towards resolving the conflicts. The two key research issues identified relate to the capacity of the states in the region to reconcile the fragmented and incoherent institutions and systems, and the imperative to contextualise democracy to meet the needs and aspirations of local people. This paper is therefore of importance to scholars and policy actors with an interest in peace, security and development in one of Africa's most troubled sub-regions.

Cyril Obi
Senior Researcher
The Nordic Africa Institute

Introduction

The Greater Horn region is one of the most conflict-ravaged areas on the African continent.[1] The populations of the region have endured many inter-state and intra-state armed conflicts during the post-independence era, starting in 1956, when Sudan became the first sub-Saharan African country to get its independence, and the present. The region was by no means peaceful before the era of decolonisation. During the period roughly between the early 1800s and the era of decolonisation, for example, it experienced many wars, which revolved mostly around state formation and empire building; slave raids; control of resources and trade routes; colonisation and resistance to colonialism; and the liberation struggle. This paper, however, is limited to the postcolonial era.

The region presently consists of seven countries, including Djibouti, Eritrea, Ethiopia, Kenya, Somalia, Sudan and Uganda, which are members of the Inter-governmental Authority for Development (IGAD),[2] plus Southern Sudan, which became independent on 9 July 2011 and is the latest addition to the region. If Somaliland, which has declared its independence from the rest of Somalia, achieves international recognition as an independent state, the number of countries in the region will increase to nine. However, it should be noted that the fragmentation of Sudan into north and south is likely to add to the region's instability, as will be explained later.

Although interconnected, the region's conflicts occur at several levels, including direct inter-state wars and armed conflicts; intra-state civil wars and conflicts; and inter-communal conflicts.[3] The distinction between wars and armed conflicts follows the differentiation drawn by the Uppsala Conflict Data Program (UCDP), according to which the former involves casualty figures of 100 people and higher per year, while the latter involves casualty figures of less

---

1. The Horn of Africa proper is a geographical concept referring to the countries of Djibouti, Eritrea, Ethiopia, and Somalia. The Greater Horn, on the other hand, is largely a political concept that incorporates Kenya, Sudan, and Uganda into the Horn region and encompasses all the countries of the Intergovernmental Authority for Development (IGAD).

2. At the time of writing, Eritrea had suspended its membership of IGAD due to disagreements over IGAD's support for Ethiopia's invasion of Somalia in 2006 to remove the Islamic Courts Union (ICU) from power.

3. The divide between inter-state and intra-state conflicts is not always clear, especially in cases of contested sovereignty. It is, for example, unclear whether border clashes between Somaliland and Pun land is an inter-state or intra-state conflict. It was also controversial whether Eritrea's war of independence was an intra-state or an inter-state conflict, since, from the point of view of Eritrean nationalists, the war was in reaction to Ethiopia's illegal annexation of their country. For the purposes of this paper, only wars between UN-recognised sovereign states are referred as inter-state wars.

than 100 per year but more than 25.[4] Lack of reliable data on casualty figures, however, does not always allow strict adherence to this differentiation.

This study has two principal objectives. One is to examine the factors that have contributed to the violent conflicts, paying special attention to those that have received little consideration in the existing literature. The second objective is to explain why the region is likely to remain a major conflict zone unless some critical structural and institutional changes are undertaken both at national and regional levels. The paper is organised into four sections. The first section sketches a conceptual framework for organising the analysis of the complex factors that have engendered the region's different levels of violent conflict. The second part identifies the main conflicts in each of the three categories by examining the key factors that have produced them and discussing some of their human and material costs. The third section proffers explanations for the region's chronic conflicts and why the conflicts are likely to endure. In particular, the conflict-engendering contextual and core factors driving the violence are addressed. The concluding section attempts to identify areas of research that can inform the search for peaceful transformation of the region.

Theoretical Framework

The large number of intricately interwoven factors that engender the region's three levels of conflict make it challenging to chart a theoretical framework that captures their complexity. The core factors revolve around the nature of the postcolonial state and the structures of governance associated with it, both at domestic and regional levels. The contextual factors, by contrast, refer to the various inherited or externally imposed socioeconomic settings and rapidly deteriorating environmental conditions under which the states of the region operate. The working proposition is that a combination of core and contextual factors produces the conflicts, and bringing peace to the region requires addressing both groups of factors at the domestic and regional levels.

This conceptual anchor allows us to do three things. First, it enables us to examine (a) the contextual conditions left behind by precolonial empires and the colonial state; (b) the conditions and constraints that continue to be imposed on the region by the contemporary global system, including the various types of external intervention; and (c) the havoc that the rapid environmental degradation is wreaking on the region. Second, it enables us to explain why the governments of the region uniformly fail to produce noteworthy success in diversity

---

4. Different data sets, such as the Correlates of War (COW) and International Peace Institute in Oslo (PRIO), use different casualty thresholds.

management, nation-building and in advancing democratic governance, which are essential for bringing the conflicts under control. The region's governments have failed in cultivating these conditions, despite differences in their ideological persuasions and in their governance systems. The failure of all of them in this regard cries out for explanation. Third, it provides an opportunity to address the gaps in the literature on the conflicts of the Greater Horn by placing emphasis on neglected factors. The literature on the Horn and its conflicts is rather extensive. The impacts of many aspects of the colonial legacy, the predatory nature of the state, the unaccountable governance and the ethnocratic and self-serving characteristics of the leadership are among the issues that have received extensive coverage. However, the direct and indirect impacts on the region's conflicts of some critical contextual factors, such as the lingering fragmentation of the modes of production and institutional systems, are essentially ignored.

The countries of the Horn, like most other African countries, are characterised by fragmented economic and institutional systems. The economic systems in the subsistence peasant and pastoral communities and those that the state and the modern sector operate under are often incompatible. The institutional systems that correspond to the different economic systems are also different. Customary land ownership rights and resource allocation mechanisms, as well as the systems of adjudication and resolution of conflicts in the two spheres, are disharmonious and represent different economic, political and cultural spaces. Such fragmentation of the political space exposes the segments of the population adhering to traditional economic and institutional systems to economic and political marginalisation, as is evident from the disproportionately high poverty rates and low access to public service among the peasant and pastoral communities. How governance works in such divided socioeconomic spaces is a critical question, barely touched in the existing literature. The governments of the region have also shown little indication that they have fully grasped the constraints on governance imposed by the fragmentation of the socioeconomic spaces. They continue to largely ignore customary property rights laws, resource-allocation mechanisms and conflict-resolution systems when, in most cases, the overwhelming majority of their populations are governed by customary institutions.[5] To their credit, however, some of the governments are beginning to address the issue, albeit in a limited way. The Ethiopian government, for example, seems to have realised that its formal system of conflict adjudication is incapable of providing adequate service to the population in rural areas and there are signs

---

5.   A recent four-country study by Mengisteab, Hagg, et al. (2011) shows that an overwhelming majority of survey respondents in rural and peri-urban areas (71.2% in South Africa, 65% in Kenya, 59.2% in Somaliland and 78.7% in Ethiopia) take intra-community conflicts to traditional institutions instead of to formal courts for settlement.

it might be exploring ways of incorporating the traditional (informal) systems operating in rural communities.

It is questionable that traditional conflict-adjudication can be incorporated effectively without the incorporation of the customary law on property rights. There is also little research to inform policy on how the parallel systems can be harmonised. Given the magnitude of the country's land-based conflicts, Kenya's recently ratified constitution also represents progress in recognising community ownership of land. If properly implemented, Article 63 of the constitution affirms that communal land belongs to the community, which suggests that customary ownership of land will be recognised and protected. This paper's contribution to the literature lies in its attempt to initiate discussion and research that would grapple with the issue of fragmented socioeconomic systems and their direct and indirect contribution to the region's conflicts.

The Region's Major Wars and Conflicts: Inter-State Wars and Conflicts

The Horn of Africa has experienced more inter-state wars than any other region on the continent. It has seen four major inter-state wars and at least three violent conflicts in the post-independence era. The major wars were fought primarily but not exclusively over territorial and border disputes. Contextual factors have played a major role in inter-state wars, since the boundaries of the countries of the region were established by precolonial empires (such as the Abyssinian Empire6 in present day Ethiopia and the Mahdiyya state in present day Sudan) and the colonial state. The wars over the Ogaden, the Ethiopia-Eritrea war (1960-91) and the Southern Sudanese war (1956–72; 1983–2005) cannot be explained without reference to their contextual roots, which go back to the precolonial empires and the colonial state. However, these wars cannot be fully explained by the contextual factors alone, since effective domestic and regional governance by the postcolonial state could have managed them without resort to violence.[7]

---

6. The name Abyssinia comes from the term Habesha, which collectively refers to people in Ethiopia and Eritrea who speak Semitic languages. While ancient empires, such as that of Axum, may have been built by the Habesha, the Abyssinian Empire usually refers to the empire which came into existence in present-day Ethiopia in the early 13th century AD. That empire largely disintegrated into small kingdoms in the 18th century and was reconstituted in the mid-19th century and expanded southwards, incorporating large groups of non-Habesha populations into the empire. The name of the country was changed from Abyssinia to Ethiopia in the aftermath of the Second World War to reflect the new demographic composition of the empire.

7. It is often argued that border disputes do not lead to war and that it is unaccountable governance that causes border wars (see Samatar and Machaka 2006). Our agreement with such claim is qualified. It is true that border disputes do not necessarily lead to wars since they can be managed peacefully. However, since wars often are the failure of politics, the same argument can be made about most wars. Non-state actors have also been major instigators of inter-state conflicts in the region.

Among the region's major wars are the three fought between Ethiopia and Somalia. The first, over Somalia's claims to the Somali-inhabited Ogaden region of Ethiopia, started in 1961, escalated in 1964 and lingered until 1967 as low intensity conflict. The second Ethiopia-Somalia war, again fought over the Ogaden problem, took place between 1977 and 1978 and involved direct external intervention, including troops and technical advisors from Cuba and the USSR in support of Ethiopia. Defeat in that war largely precipitated the collapse of the Somali state in 1991. The third war between the two countries occurred between 2006 and 2009. After a decade and half of statelessness, Somalia appeared to have re-established the state under the Islamic Courts Union (ICU), which brought most of Somalia under its control in June 2006. Ethiopia, however, viewed the ICU's Islamist rhetoric and stated aspirations of uniting all Somalis under one state as a threat to its stability and territorial integrity. As a result, it intervened preemptively to dislodge the ICU from power and to support the Transitional Federal Government (TFG), which had been ineffective since its constitution in 2004 in Nairobi as Somalia's government.[8] Ethiopia's invasion was supported by the US, which also had concerns over the ICU's Islamist rhetoric and viewed some of the ICU's leaders as having connections with Al-Qaida. The head of the council of the ICU, Hassan Dahir Aweys, for example, was included on the list of 189 individuals and organisations designated terrorist under Executive Order 13224 in the wake of 9/11.

Ethiopian troops succeeded in removing the ICU from power but could not pacify Somalia. The TFG, which rode on the tails of Ethiopian troops to power, enjoyed little legitimacy in Somalia. It was widely viewed as a creation of outside powers and largely made up of warlords who had divided up the country into small fiefs. In the wake of the removal of the ICU from power, a more radical Islamist insurgency group, *al Shebab,* emerged and, along with the remnants of the ICU under a new name, Alliance for the Re-Liberation of Somalia (ARS), continued to fight the TFG and Ethiopian troops. With the latter unable to defeat the insurgency and the TFG's position becoming increasingly untenable, the UN brokered negotiations between the TFG and a "moderate" wing of the ARS[9] (ARS-Djibouti) in Djibouti. The negotiations resulted in agreements to form a TFG-ARS unity government and the withdrawal of Ethiopian troops from Somalia. The unity government was led by the former chairman of the ICU, Sheik Ahmed Sherif, and was formed in December 2009. Like the first

---

8. The TFG replaced a Transitional National Government (TNG), which was formed in Arta, Djibouti in 2000. The TNG was opposed by a coalition called the Somali Restoration and Reconciliation Council (SRRC), which was supported by Ethiopia and led by Abdullahi Yusuf, who became the president of Somalia under the TFG.

9. The ARS leadership, which had been in exile in Asmara after being dislodged from power by Ethiopian troops, split into a "moderate" wing (ARS-Djibouti) and a "radical" wing (ARS-Asmara).

TFG, this new government has been rejected by groups who did not participate in the negotiations. The *al Shebab* and the more "radical" wing of the ARS (ARS-Asmara), now known as *Hizbul Islamiya*, led by Sheik Hassan Dahir Aweys, have continued to fight to topple the new government. Despite support from AU peacekeepers (AMISOM), diplomatic support from the UN and military and diplomatic support from the US, Ethiopia and other regional governments, Uganda and Kenya in particular, the TFG has been unable to defeat the insurgency groups. Like the first TFG, the second TFG remains ineffective and owes its existence to external powers. The country's civil war, however, continues to ravage the population.

The 1998–2000 border war between Ethiopia and Eritrean is perhaps the largest war the region has seen in the post-decolonisation era, at least in terms of casualty figures. A border dispute in the environs of Badme, a small town on the border between southwestern Eritrea and northwestern Ethiopia, escalated into a fully fledged war in May 1998. In December 2000, the Algiers Treaty was signed ending the war and establishing the Eritrea-Ethiopia Boundary Commission, which was tasked with demarcating the boundary between the two countries. On 13 April 2002, the commission gave its ruling, which delineated the entire border between the two countries on the basis of colonial treaties. By its ruling, the town of Badme, the flashpoint of the war, was placed in Eritrea, but Ethiopia, despite reluctantly accepting the commission's ruling, has yet to allow the demarcation of the boundary on the ground. In the absence of such progress, the commission declared its task completed after a virtual demarcation of the border. However, the border problem remains unsettled, since Ethiopia has neither allowed physical demarcation nor accepted the virtual demarcation.

In addition to the above four major wars, the region has also seen smaller inter-state conflicts. The Kenya-Somalia conflict during Kenya's Shifta wars (1963–67) is one such conflict. Uganda and Sudan also experienced armed conflicts and tense relations over accusations of support for each other's rebel groups. With the coming to power in Kampala in 1986 of the National Resistance Movement (NRM), which had close ties with the Sudan People's Liberation Movement (SPLM), Sudan resorted to supporting Uganda's rebel groups, including the Allied Democratic Forces (ADF) and the Lord's Resistance Army (LRA), in retaliation for Uganda's alleged support of SPLM. A brief border scrimmage between Eritrea and Djibouti in June 2008 is another of the region's inter-state conflicts. At the time of writing, the Eritrea-Djibouti border dispute remained unsettled, although a Qatar-led mediation has succeeded in deescalating the conflict and in achieving the withdrawal of Eritrean troops from the contested areas.

Other contentious but currently dormant border issues in the region include those between Uganda and Kenya, between Kenya and Sudan over the Elemi triangle and those between Ethiopia and Sudan. These unsettled issues have not precipitated violent conflicts yet but future conflicts cannot be entirely ruled out. With South Sudan breaking away from the rest of the country, border problems between the two Sudans is likely to prove more challenging, especially since the contested areas include important sources of oil.

The countries of the Horn have also fought many proxy wars against each other by engaging in what Cliffe (2002:54) calls "mutual interference", that is, support for each other's insurgency movements. However, since the insurgents in most cases are domestic forces, these conflicts are discussed under intra-state conflicts.

Intra-State Wars and Conflicts

Every country in the region has faced at least one civil war during the postcolonial era. In most cases, states have fought multiple civil wars, with the parties to the conflict the state or militia groups created by the state on the one side and sub-state actors, such as ethnic, regional, religious or other political organisations on the other.[10]

The region's civil wars differ in scope and intensity and many of them are closely linked to inter-state conflicts, since in many cases the groups that fight against the state either serve as proxies for other states or are supported by them. Governments in the Greater Horn have intervened in each other's internal conflicts for a variety of reasons. Some support insurgencies in a neighbouring country because of ethnic ties with the rebelling groups. It is also not uncommon for ethnic-based insurgency groups to obtain support from populations of neighbouring countries because of ethnic ties, even when they do not obtain direct support from governments of those neighbouring countries. Insurgency movements in Ethiopia's Somali-inhabited Ogaden region, such as the Western Somalia Liberation Front (WSLF), for example, were supported by the Somali state before its collapse in 1991.[11] The Shifta wars in Kenya's Somali-inhabited North Eastern Province were also backed by the Somali state, which aspired to unite all Somali-inhabited areas in the region under the Somali state.

In other cases, regimes have supported rebel groups in a neighbouring country as extensions of their foreign policies, including destabilisation of regimes they have antagonistic relations with. Ethiopia and Kenya responded to what they perceived as a Somali threat to their national integrity by establishing a

---

10. Civil wars are distinguished from one-sided wars, which are wars states wage against political opponents, by the casualty figures the non-state side is able to inflict on the forces of the state. The threshold is usually 100 deaths per year (see Cramer 2006).

11. The Ogaden is now part of the Somali state (Zone 5) of the Ethiopian federal state.

mutual defence pact in 1964. Moreover, successive Ethiopian regimes countered Somalia's support for irredentist movements by aiding insurgency movements such as the Somali National Movement (SNM) and Somali Salvation Democratic Front (SSDF) against the Somali state to weaken its ability to pursue its claims over the Ogaden. As noted above (see footnote 8), in the early 2000s Ethiopia supported the Somali Restoration and Reconciliation Council (SRRC) against the Transitional National Government. Presently Ethiopia supports the TFG against the *al Shebab-Hizbul Islamiya* insurrection.

Sudan supported Eritrea's liberation movements, the People's Liberation Front (EPLF) and the Eritrean Liberation Front (ELF). It also supported the Tigray People's Liberation Front against the regime of Mengistu Haile Mariam of Ethiopia. Ethiopia, for its part, supported the SPLM against successive Sudanese regimes. Uganda also supported the SPLM while Sudan reciprocated by supporting Uganda's LRA and other Ugandan rebel groups. Sudan supported the Eritrean Islamic Jihad in 1993–94 and Eritrea reciprocated by supporting Sudan's opposition groups, the National Democratic Alliance (Kibreab 2009). Eritrea currently is said to support various Ethiopian insurgency groups against the Ethiopian regime, while the Ethiopian regime retaliates by supporting Eritrean opposition groups, including the Eritrean Democratic Alliance and other smaller groups, such as the Red Sea Afar Democratic Organisation (RSADO). Eritrea is also accused by the UN Security Council, the US government, the African Union and IGAD of supporting Somali insurgency groups against the TFG as an extension of its conflict with Ethiopia, although little evidence has been disclosed on Eritrea's military support to the Somali insurgency. Some analysts, such as the International Crisis Group, for example, dismiss the alleged links between Eritrea and the Somali insurgent group *al Shebab* (Onyiego 2010).

The civil wars in the region are not simply products of proxy engagements by other states, however. Despite their engagement in such wars against each other, the region's regimes have also cooperated in curbing the activities of each other's insurgencies. Emperor Haile Selassie's Ethiopia, for example, agreed not to support the SPLM in return for Sudan's pledge not to support Eritrea's liberation movements (Kibreab 2009). Before their border war, Ethiopia and Eritrea also cooperated against rebel groups in Ethiopia's Afar region. Sudan and Eritrea have presently stopped supporting each other's rebels. Southern Sudan has also cooperated with Uganda against the LRA.

Many of the civil wars are triggered by domestic factors, such as problems of diversity management and nation-building, including the real or perceived uneven development and ethnocratic characteristics of the state, even though some form of external intervention might be involved. Others are reactions to repressive rule and ineffective governance, while yet others are triggered by intra-elite power struggles. As Deng (1995) notes, intra-elite rivalry often leads to interethnic rivalries. A few were triggered by ideological disputes. The Ethiopian People's Revolutionary Party (EPRP), a leftist organisation, which fought the military government in the late 1970s, is an example.

The collapse of the Somali state in 1991 resulted, at least in part, from the country's civil wars. Since the collapse, the country has endured wars among various warlords, 1991–2006; in Puntland against the fragile state of Somalia, 2004; ICU vs. The Alliance for the Restoration of Peace and Counter-Terrorism (ARPCT), 2006; TFG vs. ICU, 2005–06; TFG against the *al Shebab* and *Hizbul Islamiya*, 2009-present.

Sudan has perhaps faced the most deadly civil wars in terms of casualty figures. Among Sudan's most important wars are the North-South war of 1955–72; the North-South war of 1983–2005; the Darfur Conflict, 2003–present; the Beja Congress and the Rashaida Free Lions of the East; and rebellion of the Nuba mountain region.

Ethiopia has encountered the greatest number of civil-wars in the region. Among the most prominent are those against the Eritrea liberation movements, 1961–91; the Tigrai People's Liberation Front (TPLF), 1975–91; the Western Somali Liberation Front (WSLF), 1974–78; the Oromo Liberation Front, 1975–present; the Afar Liberation Front, 1975–97; and the Ogaden National Liberation Front, 1984–present. There have also been many other smaller liberation fronts that operated against the state at one time or another, including one of the few ideologically based conflicts, that involving the EPRP, 1975–77.

Kenya has faced relatively fewer wars, although it has not been immune to the factors that have engendered such conflicts, as is evident from the 1992 violence which led to approximately 2,000 deaths and 500,000 displaced persons (APRM Kenya 2006). The 2007 post-election violence that rocked the country resulted in the death of about 1,300 people and the displacement of over 600,000. The government of the People's Rally for Progress in Djibouti has also faced insurgency from an Afar organisation, The Front for the Restoration of Unity and Democracy (FRUD), 1991–94. FRUD continued to engage in low intensity conflict between 1994 and 2001. Uganda also has faced a number of civil wars waged by various armed groups. Among them are the Buganda war of 1966; the wars during the regime of Idi Amin (1972–79); the wars waged by the Ugandan National Rescue Front against the Obote government, 1980–85; the National Resistance Army, 1982-86; the Uganda Peoples Democratic Army (UPDA), 1986–88; the Allied Democratic Forces (ADF), 1996–present; and the LRA, which emerged in 1987. The war against the LRA continues to destabilise the country.

Like the inter-state wars, the civil wars also have both contextual and core factors. Precolonial empires and the colonial state left behind ethnic identities fragmented in several states, fragmented economic and institutional systems and uneven socioeconomic development among regions and ethnic groups. These conditions have made diversity management and nation-building difficult. As will be explained in the next section, the postcolonial state and regional governance have done little to correct the inherited legacies and have often exacerbated the problems.

Inter-Communal Conflicts

In addition to civil wars, Horn countries have faced many inter-communal armed conflicts. These are often fought between ethnic and clan groups over resources such as land, water and even livestock. While not limited to pastoralists, these conflicts tend to affect such communities disproportionately. In some cases, governments aggravate the conflicts by interfering on one side or the other, as the cases of Darfur in Sudan and Gambella in Ethiopia show. If certain identity groups engage in rebellion or resist policy measures, governments tend to intervene in communal conflicts by supporting rival identity groups. In other cases, inter-communal competition over resources may intensify into deadly conflicts, due to government inability to address such conflicts in a timely manner. Countless inter-communal conflicts, which have often intensified with the availability of small arms, have contributed to instability and economic disruptions in the region. Undoubtedly, these conflicts are sporadic and of much lower intensity than inter-state and civil wars. Yet because of their frequency, they are highly destructive. South Sudan's inter-communal conflicts in Jonglei area, for example, are estimated to have resulted in over 2,500 deaths and the displacement of some 350,000 people in 2009 alone (BBC News online, 22 January 2010). Ethiopia's inter-communal conflicts include those between: Afar-Issa identities (2002); Afar-Kereyou (2002–03); Amaro-Guji (2006); Anuak-Dinka (2002); Anuak-Nuer (2002–03); Bi'idyahan-Ismail (2003); Borana-Guji (2006); Borana-Konso (2008); Burji-Guji (2006); Dawa-Gura, (2003); Derashe-Konso (2008); Dizi-Surma (2002); Gabra-Guji (2005); Gumuz-Oromo (2008); Majerteen-Ogaden (2004); Marehan-Majerteen (2006); Merille-Turkana (2005); Murle-Nuer (2006); Nyangatom, Toposa-Turkana (2006); Ogaden-Sheikal (2002); and Oromo-Somali.

Kenya's inter-communal conflicts include: Borana-Gabra (2005); Dongiro-Turkana (2006); Garre-Murle (2005, 2008); Kalenjin-Kikuyu (2008); Kalenjin-Kisii (2008); Luo-Kikuyu (2008); Nyangatom-Turkana (2008); Pokot-Turkana (2006, 2008); and Topsa-Turkana (2008). Among Sudan's inter-communal conflicts are: Aqar (Dinka)-Aqok (Dinka) (2006); Ereigat Abbala Arabs-Zaghawa (2002); Habaniya-Falata (2007); Habaniya-Rizeigat Baggara (2006); Hotiya Baggara-Newiba, Mahariba and Mahamid (2005); Missiriya-Rizeigat Baggara (2008);

Murle-Bor Dinka (2007); Murle-Nuer Lou (2006); Nuer Lou-Hol Dinka (2008); Rizeigat Baggara-Ma'aliyah (2002, 2004); Terjam-Rizeigat Abbala (2007); Toposa-Didinga (2007); and between the Zaghawa and Ma'aliya (2008). Somalia and Uganda have also had a sizeable number of inter-communal conflicts.

Human and Material Costs of the Wars

Estimates of casualty figures from the various post-independence wars and armed conflicts of the region are highly unreliable and in some cases non-existent. From anecdotal estimates, however, the direct and indirect casualty figures are frighteningly high. Casualty figures from Sudan's first North-South conflict (1955–72) are put at 500,000.[12] The second North-South civil war of the Sudan (1983–2005) is said to have produced some 2 million dead, 420,000 refugees and over 4 million displaced. According to various estimates, the casualty figures for the Darfur conflict are estimated at over 180,000, with roughly 2 million people displaced. Human rights organisations estimate the Darfur casualty figures to be over 300,000 deaths (Qugnivet 2006).[13] Eritrea's casualties from its war of independence (1961–91) are estimated to be around 50,000. Casualty figures for Ethiopia's various wars between 1962 and 1992 are estimated at about 1.4 million (Twentieth Century Atlas, not dated). The Ethiopian-Eritrean border war of 1998–2000 is estimated to have claimed between 70,000 and 120,000 lives and resulted in the displacement of hundreds of thousands of people. Estimated casualty figures for the Ogaden war between Ethiopia and Somalia (1996–98) exceed 31,000, while the estimates for the ongoing Somali civil wars since 1991 range between 300,000 and 400,000. Indeed, since the start of 2007 alone, Somalia's civil wars are believed to have led to 18,000 deaths and the displacement of over 1.4 million people, while Ethiopia's invasion of Somalia in 2006 resulted in over 8,500 deaths. Uganda's conflict with Buganda in 1966 is said to have left 2,000 dead and the wars in Uganda during Idi Amin's rule (1972–79) produced some 300,000 deaths. A similar number died during Uganda's civil wars (1979–86), with roughly 750,000 people displaced, and the country's conflicts against the LRA since 1987 are said to have cost between 2,000 and 5,000 deaths. As noted above, Kenya's 2007 post-election violence led to the deaths of roughly 1,300 people. No doubt, the various inter-communal conflicts continue to add to the casualty figures.

---

12. The estimates of casualty figures are extracted from the various estimates compiled in the Twentieth Century Atlas-Death Tolls and Casualty Statistics for Secondary Wars and Atrocities, http://users.erols.com/mwhite28/warstat3.htm

13. The government of Sudan strongly disagrees with this estimate of casualties. Its own estimate is in the tens of thousands only.

The conflicts have also made the region one of the largest sources of refugees in the world, estimated in 2008 at 1,248,565, with about 8.5 million internally displaced (World Bank 2008; UNDP 2008). In addition, the region's conflicts have led to gross human rights abuses. The region's governments are often accused by human rights organisations of atrocities against citizens including disappearances, torture, incarceration of political opponents and journalists without due process of law, intimidation of candidates of opposition parties, as well as rigging elections (see various reports from Amnesty International; Human Rights Watch; Reporters without Borders).

The economic costs of the various wars and conflicts are also likely to be huge given the massive destruction of property and profound socioeconomic disruptions. Some view the conflicts as the single greatest barrier to the region's socio-economic development (Mwaura, Baechler and Kiplagat 2002). Unfortunately, few comprehensive estimates of the economic costs of the wars exist. Anecdotal evidence gives us some indication, however. The border war with Eritrea is, for example, said to have cost Ethiopia over $2.5 billion, while estimates of the costs for Eritrea range from $500 million to $1.5 billion. Uganda also puts its war costs over the 1986–2002 period at $1.33 billion, roughly 3 per cent of its GDP (APRM Uganda Report 2009). There are estimates of military expenditures as a ratio of gross domestic product, which give us some indication of changes in expenditure during periods of major war and periods of relative stability. However, they provide little information on the actual costs of all three levels of the conflicts, especially the economic costs to civilian populations. Similarly, military expenditures as a ratio of total public expenditures (Table 1) only give us a partial picture, since they do not reflect direct and indirect costs of the conflicts to the general population. It is, however, safe to assume that the costs of the various conflicts are large enough to make notable differences to the region's development.

Table 1. Military expenditures as a ratio of total public expenditures

Country	Djibouti	Eritrea	Ethiopia	Kenya	Somalia	Sudan	Uganda
% of government expenditure allocated to Health (1998–2007)	NA	NA	1	7	1	1	2
% of government expenditure allocated to Education (1998–2007)	NA	NA	5	26	2	8	15
% of government expenditure allocated to Defence (1998–2007)	13.6* 1995–2005	34.88* 1995–2003	17	6	38	28	26

Source: US State Department. World Military Expenditures and Arms Transfers, 1995–2005. *Source:* UNICEF, Information by Country March, 2010. http://www.unicef.org/infobycountry/

Factors in the Wars and Conflicts

As noted above, the factors that generate the Horn's conflicts are many and complex. This section elaborates on a combination of the contextual and core factors that account for the conflicts. We first deal with the contextual factors, which can be viewed as having three dimensions. One dimension relates to the socioeconomic structures and institutional systems left behind by precolonial empires and the colonial state. The second refers to the ongoing influences by the global system, including economic, political and military interventions by external powers. The third aspect refers to the rapidly deteriorating environmental conditions, which along with rapid population growth have generated scarcity of resources and conflicts among communities. The core factors refer to the nature of the postcolonial state and its governance systems. This factor also has two dimensions, including domestic governance and regional governance. We first examine each of the three dimensions of the contextual factors.

Legacies of Precolonial Empires and the Colonial State

A number of developments and socioeconomic arrangements and inter-identity power relations left behind by precolonial empires and the colonial state have become critical sources of conflict in the postcolonial era. Two notable precolonial empires in the region were the Abyssinian Empire and the Mahdiyya state in the Sudan. Both empires left behind imprints that still contribute to conflicts in the region. The Abyssinian Empire is credited with creating the modern Ethiopian state through expansionist conquests during the second half of the 19th century and defence against European colonialism. However, it also left behind inter-state boundary problems and deep disparities in citizenship rights within the country. The populations in the newly incorporated southern parts of the country were ravaged by slave raids, looting and, in many cases, large-scale land expropriations during and in the aftermath of their incorporation into the empire. Those who lost their land were reduced to landless tenants, who tilled the land for northern landlords (Pankhurst 1968).[14] The Empire also established a hierarchy of cultures, non-Abyssinian cultures in the newly incorporated territories being placed in a subordinate position. Some of the legacies of the Empire, like the landlessness created by land expropriation, have largely been reversed by the 1975 land reform. The cultural inequalities have also been mitigated with

---

14. The Abyssinian Empire played a double role in the slave trade. It curtailed the slave trade by the Oromo kingdoms, which it conquered in the late 1880s, giving relief to the victims of those kingdoms in the southern parts of the country. At the same time, however, it engaged in the slave trade itself.

the institution of a federal system in the country's 1994 constitution. However, disparities in access to political and economic power remain important sources of conflict, as is evident from the activities of the Oromo Liberation Front and the Ogaden National Liberation Front. Similarly, Sudan's Mahdiyya state, which professed Arab identity and was supported by slave-raiding communities, left behind complex scars in inter-identity relations, particularly between northern and southern identity groups, which have led the country to the brink of disintegration (Deng 2010).

The conflict-fostering legacies of precolonial empires were compounded by the structural and institutional mechanisms established by the colonial state. Four critical conflict-fomenting legacies of the latter can be identified. One is the division of various ethnic groups among a number of states. State boundaries often are arbitrary and few states in the world are made up of single ethnic groups. The degree of arbitrariness of boundaries and the resulting fragmentation of ethnic groups, however, seems disproportionately high in Africa, where states are mostly colonial creations. Table 2 provides a list of some of the ethnic groups spread across several states in the Greater Horn region. Often, the fragmentation of ethnic groups involves not only disruption of social and cultural ties but also of economic process, by hindering the movement of communities, which rely on regional ecosystems for survival, as Samatar (2006) notes. While the fragmentation of the Somali people, which led to three major wars between Ethiopia and Somalia, is the most conspicuous problem, many of the other fragmented ethnic groups have had problems with their states (see Table 2).[15] Fragmentation of ethnic groups raises citizenship and identity problems and in many cases has also led to the marginalisation of those groups.

A second legacy of colonialism is the problem of boundaries and in some cases territories. In many instances colonial boundaries are not demarcated on the ground or even clearly delineated. This vagueness has caused a number of border disputes. The Eritrea-Ethiopia border war was the greatest of these, but border disputes are rampant. As noted in the preceding section, every country in the region has border disputes with at least two of its neighbours. A border problem is likely to arise between north and South Sudan. Although the British kept South Sudan apart from the north for most of the colonial period, the boundaries between the two remain unclear and are likely to be challenging. Border conflicts are mostly inter-state conflicts, but also have serious implications for state-identity and inter-identity relations, as they entail various hardships for border communities, especially when their loyalty to their states is questioned. The Misseriya and Dinka Ngok identities in Sudan's Abyei region, for example,

---

15. The claim here is not that ethnic fragmentation by itself is a sufficient condition to lead to conflicts. Rather, it is that fragmentation often exposes groups to marginalisation, which, in turn, propels them to resist.

Table 2. A selected list of ethnic groups that are spread across different countries

Name of Ethnic Groups	Countries of Habitation	Occurrences of conflict
Afar	Djibouti*, Eritrea, Ethiopia*	Yes
Somali	Somalia*, Djibouti*, Ethiopia*, Kenya*	Yes
Luo	Kenya*, Uganda, Sudan*, Ethiopia, Tanzania	Yes
Luhya	Kenya, Uganda, Tanzania	No
Beja, Rashaida, Tigre	Eritrea and Sudan*	Yes (Beja)
Tigrigna, Kunama, Shaho (Irob)	Eritrea* and Ethiopia*	Yes
Oromo	Ethiopia* and Kenya	Yes
Pokot and Teso	Kenya and Uganda	No
Kakwa, Sebei, Lugbwara, Madi, Ancholi, Kaliko, Pojullo	Uganda* and South Sudan*	Yes
Anuak, Nuer, Bertha, Donyiro, Tirma, Shita, Gumuz, Murle, Kichepo, Wetawit	Ethiopia* and Sudan*	Yes
Daasanach	Ethiopia, Kenya and Sudan	No

*Countries where the conflicts have occurred.

are likely to have conflicting positions on South Sudan's independence and on whether Abyei forms part of the north or the south.

Another legacy of colonialism is the uneven development among regions and ethnic groups within countries. One of the key objectives of colonialism was the extraction of resources. Areas rich in mineral resources and those with fertile land in accessible locations were targets for investment, while areas deemed not profitable were generally marginalised. The Buganda areas of southern Uganda were privileged relative to the rest of the country (Mutibwa 2008). In Kenya also the British identified central Kenya and the Rift Valley area as profitable, while the western and northeastern regions, viewed as unprofitable and trouble-some, were marginalised (APRM Kenya Report 2006; Mwaura, Baechler and Kiplagat 2002). Southern Sudan and northern Uganda were among other areas relatively marginalised by the colonial state.[16] All these areas remain marginal-ised and they have become centres of conflict.

A fourth legacy of colonialism, largely absent from the literature but difficult to overcome, is the fragmentation of modes of production and the correspond-ing institutions of governance. The colonial state created a small modern capital-

---

16. There are widespread arguments that ethnic conflicts are essentially caused by an entrepreneurial elite that mobilises ethnic groups to further its own political interests. These arguments, however, tend to overstate the case. In many cases, ethnic groups rebel against the state because they face marginalisation. In such cases, the conflict cannot be simply attributed to political entrepreneurs.

ist economic sector and introduced its own institutions of governance without replacing indigenous institutions. It also did not create organic links between the two sectors such that the new sector facilitates the transformation of the traditional. Instead, it established an incoherent political economy with parallel if largely incompatible systems. As noted already, the parallel modes of production and institutional systems represent different socioeconomic spaces, and making policy that advances the interests of both has become extremely challenging. Policy is, thus, generally geared towards the modern system, marginalising the traditional sector and the population that operates under it.

The economic marginalisation of rural inhabitants, along with the institutional detachment of the state from this large segment of the population, has in many cases adversely affected the legitimacy of the state and state-society relations. Often, the marginalisation of rural inhabitants affects some ethnic (and other identity) groups more than others. Geography seems to play some role in this regard. The further an ethnic group is from urban centres, the more it relies on traditional institutions and the more limited its access to public services. In any case, inequalities frequently lead to problems of diversity management and ethnic conflict, which often exacerbate the inequalities and undermine the process of nation-building.

Postcolonial Global Environment

The global environment in the postcolonial era has also contributed to the region's inter-state and intra-state conflicts, although external intervention has also been life-saving, especially during calamities. The ideology and politics of the Cold War, for example, had a significant influence on the Eritrea-Ethiopia conflict (1961-91). US strategic interests in general and its interest in inheriting a communications base left behind by Italy following the fall of its East Africa empire in 1941 was one of the factors that led to the ill-fated federation of Eritrea with Ethiopia (Okubazghi Yohannes 1991). The intensity of the Ethiopia-Somalia conflicts was also exacerbated by the rivalry of the superpowers in arming the two countries. The imposition of structural adjustment programmes through the conditionalities of the IMF and the World Bank represented another intervention that intensified social inequalities and the rift between the modern and traditional economic sectors. The post-September 11 War on Terror is another factor that has divided the countries of the region into different camps and facilitated external intervention in Somalia's civil wars. External support to regimes who profess to be partners in the War on Terror, despite their poor record on human rights and democratisation, also seems to be worsening state-society relations.

Massive Environmental Degradation

Another contextual factor that has contributed to the conflicts and instability of the region is the alarming rate of environmental degradation it has faced. Much of the region is arid or semi-arid and has over the last five or so decades faced rapid environmental degradation, manifested in frequent droughts and chronic food and water shortages. Global climate changes and various human activities, including rapid population growth, changes in land-use patterns and chronic conflict, have contributed to the environmental degradation, which has culminated in economic and social dislocation, displacement and widespread resource-based conflicts. Deteriorating environmental conditions have exerted increasing pressure on the region's populations, especially peasants and nomads, and have resulted in land and water-based communal conflicts. While Darfur is the most obvious case, many of the communal conflicts identified in this paper's second section are impacted by scarcity of resources caused by environmental degradation.

Table 3. Droughts in the Horn of Africa, 1980–2010

	Djibouti	Eritrea	Ethiopia	Kenya	Somalia	Sudan	Uganda
Total number of droughts 1980–2008	6.0	3.0	8.0	9.0	8.0	0.7	0.6
Average Number of droughts/year1980–2008	0.28	0.19	0.28	0.33	0.28	0.25	0.22

Source: EM-DAT, The International Disaster Database, http://www.emdat.be/result-country-profile

Nature and Failure of the Postcolonial State

The contextual factors represent the conditions under which the postcolonial state has to operate. No doubt, they pose serious challenges for the region's governance and peaceful socioeconomic development. However, they don't necessarily determine outcomes, since the postcolonial state and regional intergovernmental organisations can remove the obstructive conditions and transform the context. Unfortunately, the postcolonial state in the Horn, like the state on the rest of the continent, has not transformed the context.

Two types of failures characterise the state. One failure relates to the self-serving behaviour of most leaders and other functionaries of the state. Given the weakness of the political systems, leaders are often able to subordinate broad social interests to their own private interests, including monopolising political power. Often they also become ethnocratic, as Ali Mazrui (1975) notes, or they are perceived as such by large segments of the population, since they tend to rely on ethnic affiliations to secure their power. In some cases, such self-serving leaders may even perpetuate wars and ethnic/clan conflicts when they find them to be instrumental in extending their hold on power. Somalia's Siad Barre is one leader who resorted to clan politics as the legitimacy of his government waned. During the dying years of his rule, Mengistu Haile Mariam also attempted to portray the insurgency in Eritrea and Tigray as an ethnic (Tigray/Tigrigni) drive for power. Such states can hardly be expected to transform the context and bring about the regime's peaceful transformation.

The second and more general failure relates to lack of understanding of the nature of the contextual impediments and/or inability to transform them. The legacies of precolonial empires and colonial state, thus, remain largely intact. The fragmented ethnic groups in the region have seen little by way of arrangements that would help alleviate their burden. The region's ethnic groups, victims of uneven development under colonialism, continue to bear the burden of uneven development and marginalisation. Eastern and southeastern Ethiopia, southern and western Sudan, northern Uganda and western and northeastern Kenya are the most obvious examples. The postcolonial state also continues to operate on the basis of imported institutions and is largely oblivious to the institutions adhered to by most of its population. Efforts at transforming traditional modes of production and thereby at harmonising the fragmented modes of production have also been grossly inadequate. Under the prevailing institutional and economic fragmentation, neither nation-building nor viable democratisation is feasible. No doubt the countries of the region, with the exception of Eritrea and Somalia, conduct elections. Yet elections, in most cases, do not lead to changes of leader or government. The current leaders of four of the countries of the region have, for instance, been in power for almost two decades. In Uganda, the regime has been in power for 24 years, in Sudan 21 years and in Ethiopia and Eritrea, for 20 years. More importantly, elections hardly represent the segments of the population that live under the traditional modes of production and institutional systems. Rural inhabitants, of course, participate in elections but there is little to suggest that the pool of candidates they choose from represents their interests or even that rural people vote for candidates on the basis of their own interests.

Failure to transform the context by bridging the institutional divide explains why African governments fail in diversity management and nation-building and democratisation, despite differences in quality of leadership and types of government. In other words, the region's governments, regardless of their ideological orientation or even levels of commitment to national development, operate under imported institutional systems that detach the state from its populations. Despite the glaring institutional incoherence, there has been little effort to contextualise the institutions of democracy even when the rhetoric of democracy is on the rise.

Failure of Regional Governance

The failure of the region's states in transforming their socioeconomic structures and institutional systems is compounded by the failure of regional and continental intergovernmental organisations. The countries of the Greater Horn are members of IGAD, Common Market for Eastern and Southern Africa (COMESA), as well as the African Union. Yet none of these intergovernmental bodies has been effective in reducing the conflicts of the region. Although the continent is replete with border disputes, intergovernmental organisations, including the African Union, have yet to develop effective mechanisms for settling boundary disputes before they escalate into war.

These organisations have also not been able to develop mechanisms that would ease the challenge of fragmented ethnic identities. Somalia's attempts to redraw its colonial boundaries in order to unite all Somalis under one state received little support from other African states or the Organisation of African Unity (OAU) in the early 1960s. The OAU decided that colonial boundaries are sacrosanct since tampering with them was likely to open a Pandora's Box and lead to wars all over the continent.[17] Undoubtedly, redrawing colonial boundaries would be risky. However, the OAU and AU have not instituted mechanisms that would allow populations divided by national boundaries to maintain their economic and cultural ties with each other though flexible borders. Furthermore, despite the numerous conflicts the region as well as the continent face, the regional organisations as well as the African Union have yet to establish effective conflict-resolution mechanisms. Is seems the resolution of African conflicts is often outsourced to actors outside the continent.

Possible Changes and Areas of Research

The foregoing discussion suggests that bringing the region's conflicts under control requires bold and fundamental change. The border conflicts that lead to inter-state wars and conflicts can be dealt with through effective and proactive measures by regional organisations. However, to become effective a regional

---

17. The AU's policy with regard to colonial boundaries has remained intact so far. Eritrea's independence did not contravene the AU's policy since Eritrea was a colonial creation. Southern Sudan's independence, when it materialises, will be the real change to the AU's longstanding policy.

organisation such as IGAD would require a level of independence from member states as well as external powers so that it could operate as a neutral body. Moreover, since intra-state and inter-state conflicts are closely intertwined, the organisation would need to deal with both.

Regional organisations also need to chart innovative arrangements that would alleviate the burden of fragmented ethnic groups. This would require advances in the regional integration agenda so that borders are open to allow divided populations to maintain full social, cultural and economic interactions with their identity groups across borders with little hindrance. The success of regional integration schemes is, therefore, imperative not only for economic development but for internal and regional peace and stability.

Perhaps the most challenging problem the region faces is transforming the nature of the state. Much emphasis has been placed on democratisation as critical to changing the nature of the state and allowing effective management of diversity and nation-building in the region. There is little doubt that peaceful management of diversity and nation-building is unlikely to succeed without democratic governance. However, democratisation also requires reconciliation of the fragmented institutions and integration of the fragmented modes of production. Effective democratic governance under conditions of fragmented and incoherent institutional systems is hardly conceivable. Institutional reconciliation, in turn, implies contextualisation of democracy to ensure it reflects local realities and becomes relevant to the population under both institutional systems. Without institutional transformation, current democratic efforts lack the foundations to develop into genuine democratic systems that bring the marginalised segments of society into the political process.

Unfortunately, there has not been much effort towards structural and institutional transformation in the region, without which the region, sadly, is likely to remain conflict-prone for the foreseeable future. There has also not been much research undertaken into how the state can reconcile the fragmented and incoherent institutional systems. Another area where research is in acute need is on how democratic institutions can be contextualised so that the people that live under different modes of production and institutional systems can become stakeholders in the democratisation struggle.

Bibliography

Abdi, A.A., 1997, "The Rise and Fall of Somali Nationalism: From Traditional Society to Fragile 'Nationhood' to post-State", *Horn of Africa* 15(1/4):34–80.

Abbink, J., 2003, "Ethiopia-Eritrea: Proxy Wars and Prospects of Peace in the Horn of Africa", *Journal of Contemporary African Studies* 21(3):407–25.

Adams, M., 1982, "The Baggara Problem: Attempts at Modern Change in Southern Darfur and Southern Kordofan (Sudan)", *Development and Change* 13:259–89.

Adejumobi, S., 2001, "Citizenship, Rights, and the Problem of Conflicts and Civil Wars in Africa", *Human Rights Quarterly* 23:148–70.

Afric.com, 2008, "Kenya: SMS Text Messages the New Guns of War?: Fueling Hate with Cell Phone Messages", http://en.afrik.com/article12629.html (20 February).

Ahmed, A.G.M., 2001, "Livelihood and Resource Competition, Sudan", in Salih, M. et al. (eds), *African Pastoralism.* London: Pluto Press.

allAfrica.com, 24 October 2008, "Djibouti President Urges Security Council to Press. Eritrea on Ending Border Dispute". http://allafrica.com/stories/200810240561. html

Amutabi, M.N., 2005, "Transient, Mobile 'Nations' and the Dilemma of Nationhood in the Horn of Africa: Interrogating Nomadic Pastoralists, Insecurity and the Uncertainty of Belonging", in Yieke, F.A. (ed.), *East Africa in Search of National and Regional Renewal.* Dakar: CODESRIA, pp. 103–33.

Anonymous, 2002, "Government Recognition in Somalia and Regional Political Stability in the Horn of Africa", *Journal of Modern African Studies* 40(2):247–72.

African Peer Review Mechanism (APRM), 2006, *Country Review Report of the Republic of Kenya.* Addis Ababa.

—, 2009, *Country Review Report of the Republic of Uganda*, Addis Ababa.

Awuondo, O.C.,1992, *Life in the Balance: Ecological Sociology of Turkana Nomads.* Nairobi: ACTS Press.

Bariagaber, A.,2006, *Conflict and the Refugee Experience: Flight, Exile, and Repatriation in the Horn of Africa.* Aldershot: Ashgate.

Barnes, T.S.,2005, "Global Flows: Terror, Oil, and Strategic Philanthropy", *African Studies Review* 48(1) (April):1–23.

Belshaw D. and M. Malinga, 1999, "The Kalashnikov Economies of the Eastern Sahel: Cumulative or Cyclical Differentiation between Nomadic Pastoralists". Paper presented at the first workshop of the study group on conflict and security of the Development Studies Association, South Bank University. University of East Anglia.

Bereketeab, R., 2009, "The Eritrea-Ethiopia Conflict and the Algiers Agreement: Eritrea's March Down the Road to Isolation", in Reid, R. (ed.), *Eritrea's External Relations: Understanding its Role and Foreign Policy.* London: Chatham House; Washington DC: Brookings Institution Press.

Beshir, M.O.,1968, *The Southern Sudan: Background to Conflict*. London: Hurst.

Beshir, M.O., M.A.M. Salih and M.A. Abdeljalil, 1985, "Ethnicity and National Cohesion in the Sudan", special issue, *Bayreuth African Studies Series* (1).

Bollig, M., 1990, "Ethnic Conflicts in North-West Kenya: Pokot-Turkana Raiding 1969–1984", *Zeitschrift für Ethnologie* 115:73–90.

Bond, D. and P. Meier, 2006, "Resource Scarcity and Pastoral Armed Conflict in the Horn of Africa". Paper presented at the annual meeting of the International Studies Association, Town and Country Resort and Convention Center, San Diego, California, 22 March. Available online at http://www.allacademic.com/meta/ p98844_index.html.

Bondestam, L., 1974, "People and Capitalism in North Eastern Ethiopia", *Journal of Modern African Studies* 12(3):432–39.

Brons, M., 2001, *Society, Security, Sovereignty and the State in Somalia: From Statelessness to Statelessness*. Utrecht: International Books.

Bruchhaus, E-M. (ed.), 1996, *Trading Places: Alternative Models of Economic Co-operation in the Horn of Africa*. Uppsala: Life and Peace Institute.

Casper, O.A.,1990, *Life in the Balance: Ecological Sociology of Turkana Nomads*. Nairobi: ACTS.

Clapham, C., 1995a, "The Horn of Africa: A Conflict Zone", in O. Furley (ed.), *Conflict in Africa*. London: Tauris, pp. 72–91.

—, 1995b, "The Politics of Post-Insurgency", in Wiseman, J.A. (ed.), *Democracy and Political Change in Sub-Saharan Africa*. London: Routledge, pp. 116–36.

—, 1996b, "Boundary and Territory in the Horn of Africa", inNugent, P. and A.I. Asiwaju (eds), *African Boundaries: Barriers, Conduits and Opportunities*. London: Pinter, pp. 237–50.

—, 1998b, "Introduction: Analysing African Insurgencies", in Clapham, C. (ed.), *African Guerrilla*. Oxford: James Currey, pp. 1–18.

Cliffe, L., 1999, "Regional Dimension of Conflict in the Horn of Africa", *Third World Quarterly* 20(1).

—, 2004, "Regional Impact of the Eritrea-Ethiopia War", in Jacquin-Berdal, D. and M. Plaut (eds), *Unfinished Business: Ethiopia and Eritrea at War*. Trenton NJ: Red Sea Press.

Cliffe, L. and P. While, 2002, "Conflict Management and Resolution in the Horn of Africa", in Mwaura, C. and S. Schmeidl (eds), *Early Warning and Conflict Management in the Horn of Africa*. Trenton NJ: Red Sea Press.

Collier, P. and A. Hoeffler, 2000, "Greed and Grievance in Civil War", World Bank Policy Research Working Paper 2355. Washington DC: World Bank Development Research Group.

Committee to Protect Journalists, November 2005, Letter posted by the Committee to Protect Journalists (New York); Open Letter to President Museveni concerning the arrest of journalists and threat to close Newspapers that report the trial of Kiiza Besigy. http://www.cpj.org/

Connell, D., 2005, "Redeeming the Failed Promise of Democracy in Eritrea", *Race and Class* 46(4):68–79.

Cramer, C., 2006, *Civil War Is Not a Stupid Thing: Accounting for Violence in Developing Countries*. London: Hurst.

Cranna, M. (ed.), 1994, *The True Cost of Conflict*. London: Saferworld.

Daily Nation, 2008, "Role of Media in Kenya's Post Election Violence" (3 March).

Dagne, T., 2000, "The Horn of Africa: Another Humanitarian Crisis?", *Mediterranean Quarterly* (Summer).

Dagne, T. and B. Everett, 2004, Sudan: The Darfur Crisis and the Status of the North-South Negotiations. Congressional Research Service, (22 October).

Deng, F.M., 2008, *Identity, Diversity, and Constitutionalism in Africa*. Washington DC: United States Institute of Peace Press.

—, 2010, *Self-Determination and National Unity: A Challenge for Africa*. Lawrenceville NJ: Africa World Press.

Deng, L.B., 2005, "The Sudan Comprehensive Peace Agreement: Will it be Sustained?", *Civil Wars* 7(3):244–57.

Dowd, R. and M. Driessen, 2006, "Ethnically Dominated Party Systems and the Quality of Democracy: Evidence from Sub-Saharan Africa". Paper presented at the annual meeting of the American Political Science Association, Philadelphia, 31 August–3 September.

EAC, 1999, "Treaty Establishing the East African Community". Arusha: East African Community.

Eiobu, A., 2000, "Teso gets Guns from Museveni", *The Monitor*, 22 March, p. 3.

Elischer, S., 2008, "Ethnic Coalitions of Convenience and Commitment: Political Parties and Party Systems in Kenya". GIGA Research Programme: Violence, Power and Security No. 68 (February).

Englebert, P., 2000, *State Legitimacy and Development in Africa*. Boulder CO: Lynne Rienner.

Eritrea in Freedom House (n.d.) *Freedom in the World: The Annual Report of Political Rights and Civil Liberties*, http://www.freedomhouse.org/research/#reports, pp. 218–20.

Esteban, J. and D. Ray, 1994, "On the Measurement of Polarization," *Econometrica* 62 (July):819–51.

Ethiopia, Federal Democratic Republic, 1994, *Constitution of the Federal Democratic Republic of Ethiopia*. Addis Ababa: Government Printers.

Faris, S., 2007, "The Real Roots of Darfur", *Atlantic Monthly* (April).

Fessehatzion, T., 2002, *Shattered Illusion, Broken Promise: Essays on Eritrea-Ethiopia War*. Trenton NJ: Red Sea Press.

Finnstrom, S., 2006, "Wars of the Past and War in the Present: The Lord's Resistance Movement/Army in Uganda", *Africa: The Journal of the International African Institute* 76(2):200–20.

First, R., 1983, "Colonialism and the Formation of African States", in Held, D. (ed.), *States and Societies*. Oxford: Blackwell.

Flint, J. and A. de Waal, 2006, *Darfur: A Short History of a Long War.* London: Zed Books.

Foldy, E., 2004, "Learning from Diversity: A theoretical Explanation," *Public Administration Review* 64(5):529–38.

Fukui K. and J. Markakis (eds), 1994, *Ethnicity and Conflict in the Horn of Africa.* London: James Currey; Athens: Ohio University Press.

Fukui K. and D. Turton (eds), 1979, "Warfare among East African Herders", *Senri Ethnological Series*, No 3. Osaka: National Museum of Ethnology.

Gebrewold, K. and S. Byrne, 2005, "Small Arms and Light Weapons in the Horn: Reducing the Demand", in Bekoe, D.A. (ed.), *East Africa and the Horn*. New York: International Peace Academy, pp. 11–20.

Gertzel, C.J., M. Goldschmidt and D. Rothchild (eds), 1969, *Government and Politics in Kenya: A Nation Building Text*. Nairobi: East African Publishing House.

Gibert, M., 2006, "The European Union in the IGAD-Subregion: Insights from Sudan and Somalia", *Review of African Political Economy* 33(107):142–50.

Gulliver, P.H., 1955, *The Family Herds: A Study of Two Pastoral Tribes in East Africa: The Jie and Turkana*. London: Routledge and Kegan Paul.

Habte Selassie, B., 1989, *Eritrea and the United Nations and other Essays*. Trenton NJ: Red Sea Press.

Hadley J., 1997, *Pastoralist Cosmology: The Organizing Framework for Indigenous Conflict Resolution in the Horn of Africa*. Harrisonburg VA: Eastern Mennonite University.

Hamer, J., 2007, "Decentralization as a Solution to the Problem of Cultured Diversity: An Example from Ethiopia", *Africa* 77(2):207–25.

Hammond, L.C., 2003, "Obstacles to Regional Trade in the Horn of Africa: Borders, Markets, and Production", USAID.

Hansson, C., 2003, "Building New States: Lessons from Eritrea", in Addison, T. (ed.), *From Conflict to Recovery in Africa*. Oxford: Oxford University Press.

Harbeson, J.W., 1978, "Territorial and Development Politics in the Horn of Africa: The Afar of the Awash Valley", *African Affairs* 77(309) (October):479–98.

Healy, S. and M. Plaut, 2007, *Ethiopia and Eritrea: Allergic to Persuasion*. London: Chatham House.

Hedru, D., 2003, "Eritrea: Transition to Dictatorship, 1991–2003", *Review of African Political Economy* 30(97):435–44.

Hendrickson, D., R. Mearns and J. Armon, 1996, "Livestock Raiding Among the Pastoral Turkana of Kenya", *IDS Bulletin* 27(3):17–30.

Herskovits, M.J., 1952, "Some Problems of Land Tenure in Contemporary Africa", *Land Economics* 28(1) (February):37–45.

Hillharot, D. and M. van Leewen, 2005, "Grounding Local Peace Organisations: A Case of Southern Sudan", *Journal of Modern African Studies* 43(4):537–64.

ICG, 2006, "Can the Somali Crisis be Contained?" *Africa Report* No. 116 (10 August). Nairobi and Brussels: ICG.

—, 2008, "Beyond Fragile Peace between Ethiopia and Eritrea: Averting New War", *Africa Report* No. 141 (17 June).

Iyob, R. and E.J. Keller, 2005, "US Policy in the Horn: Grappling with a Difficult Legacy", in Bekoe, D.A. (ed.), *East Africa and the Horn*. New York: International Peace Academy, pp. 101–25.

Jacquin-Berdal, D. (ed.), 2005, *Unfinished Business: Ethiopia and Eritrea at War*. Trenton NJ: Red Sea Press.

Jean-Germaine, G., 1996, "Towards a Taxonomy of Failed States in the New World Order", *Third World Quarterly* 17(3):455–71.

Johnson, D., 2002, *The Root Causes of Sudan's Civil Wars*. London: James Currey.

Kabwegyere, T.B. (ed.), 1995, *The Politics of State Formation and Destruction in Uganda*. Kampala: Fountain Publishers.

Karl, T.L., 1999, "The Perils of the Petro-State: Reflections on the Paradox of Plenty", *Journal of International Affairs* 53(1):31–48.

Kasfir, N., 2005, "Sudan's Darfur: Is it Genocide?" *Current History* 104(682):195–202.

Kibreab, G., 2009, "Eritrean- Sudanese Relations in Historical Perspective", in Reid, R. (ed.), *Eritrea's External Relations: Understanding its Regional Role and Foreign Policy*. London: Chatham House.

Kendie, D.D., 1999, "Egypt and the Hydro-Politics of the Blue Nile River", *Northeast African Studies* 6(1–2):141–69 (New Series).

—, 2003, "Problems and Prospects for a Horn of Africa Confederation/Federation", *Horn of Africa* 21:1–19.

Kenworthy, J.M., 1998, "Resource Conflict in the Horn of Africa", *African Affairs* 97:579–80.

Kornprobst, M., 2002, "The Management of Border Disputes in African Regional Subsystems: Comparing West Africa and the Horn of Africa", *Journal of Modern African Studies* 40(3):369–93.

Koser, K., 2008, "Internal Displacement in Kenya". Statement by Khalid Koser, Deputy Director, Brookings-Bern Project on Internal Displacement. Brookings-Bern Project on Internal Displacement 14 March.

Laitin, D. and S.S. Samatar, 1987, *Somalia: Nation in Search of a State*. Boulder CO: Westview Press.

Lassey, A., 2000, "Mining and Community Rights – The Tarkawa Experience", *African Agenda* 2(3), Accra: Third World Network.

Lata, L., 2003, "The Ethiopia-Eritrea War", *Review of African Political Economy* (97):369–88.

—, 2004a, "Ethiopia: The Path to War, and The Consequence of Peace", in Jacquin-Berdal, D. and M. Plaut (eds), *Unfinished Business: Ethiopia and Eritrea at War*. Trenton NJ: Red Sea Press.

—, 2004b, *The Horn of Africa as Common Homeland: The State and Self Determination in the Era of Heightened Globalization*. Waterloo: Wilfred Laurier University Press.

Lewis, I. (ed.), 1983, *Nationalism and Self Determination in the Horn of Africa*. London: Ithaca Press.

Lewis, I.M., 1998, *Peoples of the Horn of Africa: Somali, Afar and Saho*. London: Haan Publishers.

—, 2002, *A Modern History of Somalia: Nation and State in the Horn of Africa*. London: Longman.

Lewis, J., 2000, *Empire State-Building: War and Welfare in Kenya 1925–1952*. Oxford: James Currey (Eastern African Studies).

Livingston, I., 1986, "The Common Property Problem and Pastoralist Economic Behaviour", *Journal of Development Studies* 23(1).

Lotuai, D., 1997, "The Causes and Consequences of Cattle Rustling among Pastoralist Communities", APA Paper No. 47/97. Nairobi: KIA.

MacInnes, C.M. (ed.), 1950, *Principles and Methods of Colonial Administration*. London: Butterworths Scientific Publications.

Mackay, J., 1982, "An Explanatory Synthesis of Primordial and Mobilizationist Approaches to Ethnic Phenomena," *Ethnic and Racial Studies*, 5(October):395–420.

Markakis, J., 1987, *National and Class Conflict in the Horn of Africa*. Cambridge: Cambridge University Press.

—, 1989, "The Ishaq-Ogaden Dispute," in Hjort af Ornäs, A. and M.A. Salih (eds), *Ecology and Politics: Environmental Stress and Security in Africa*. Uppsala: Scandinavian Institute for African Studies.

— (ed.), 1993, *Conflict and the Decline of Pastoralism in the Horn of Africa*. London: Macmillan.

—, 1998, *Resource Conflict in the Horn of Africa*. Oslo: International Peace Research Institute; London: Sage.

Maxted, J. and A. Zegeye, 2002, "Human Stability and Conflict in the Horn of Africa", *African Security Review* 11(l):55–9.

Mazrui, A., 1975, *Soldiers and Kinsmen in Uganda: the Making of a Military Ethnocracy*. Beverly Hills: Sage.

Mburu, N., 1999, "Contemporary Banditry in the Horn of Africa: Causes, History and Political Implications", *Nordic Journal of African Studies* 8(2):89–107.

Mengisteab, K., 1999, "Democratization and State Building in Africa, How Compatible Are They?", in Mengisteab, K. and C. Daddieh (eds), *State Building and Democratization in Africa*. Westpoint: Praeger, pp. 21–39.

Mengisteab, K. and C. Daddieh, 1999, "Why State Building is Still Relevant in Africa and How it Relates to Democratization", in Mengisteab, K. and C. Daddieh (eds), *State Building and Democratization in Africa*. Westpoint: Praeger, pp. 1–17.

Mengisteab, K., G. Hagg et al., 2011, "Reconciling Africa's Fragmented Institutions of Governance: A New Approach to Institution-Building". A research Report submitted to the International Development Research Center, which funded the study.

Mengisteab, K. and Y. Okbazghi, 2005, *Anatomy of the African Tragedy: Political, Economic and Foreign Policy Crisis in Post-Independence Eritrea*. Trenton NJ: Red Sea Press.

Metelis, C., 2004, "Reformed Rebels? Democratization, Global Norms and the Sudan People's Liberation Army", *Africa Today* 51(1):64–82.

Mkutu, K., 2000, "Banditry, Cattle Rustling and the Proliferation of Small Arms, the Case of Baragoi Division of Samburu District", *Arusha Report*. Nairobi: African Peace Forum.

—, 2005, "Pastoralism and Conflict in the Horn of Africa", Africa Peace Forum/ Saferworld/University of Bradford.

Mkutu, K. and M. Marani, 2001, "The Role of Civic Leaders in the Mitigation of Cattle-rustling and Small Arms: The Case of Laikipia and Samburu", Nairobi: African Peace Forum.

Möller, B., 2008, "The Horn of Africa and the US 'War on Terror' with a Special Focus on Somalia", *Post-Conflict Peace-Building in the Horn of Africa*. Lund, Research Report in Social Anthropology, 2008:1.

Morrison, J.S., 2002, "Somalia's and Sudan's Race to the Fore in Africa", *Washington Quarterly* 25(2):191–205.

Mousseau, D.Y., 2001, "Democratization with Ethnic Divisions: A Source of Conflict," *Journal of Peace Research* 38 (5):547–67.

Mudoola, D.M., 1993, *Religion, Ethnicity and Politics in Uganda*. Kampala: Fountain Publishers.

Mutibwa, P., 2008, *The Buganda Factor in Ugandan Politics*. Kampala: Fountain Publishers.

Mwaura, C. and S. Schmeidl (eds), 2002, *Early Warning and Conflict Management in the Horn of Africa*. Lawrenceville NJ and Asmara Eritrea: Red Sea Press.

Mwaura, C., G. Baechler and B. Kiplagat, 2002, "Background to Conflicts in the IGAD Region," in Mwaura, C. and S. Schmeidl (eds), *Early Warning and Conflict Management in the Horn of Africa*. Lawrenceville NJ and Asmara Eritrea: Red Sea Press.

Ndegwa, S.N., 2003, "Kenya: Third Time Lucky?", *Journal of Democracy* 14(3):145–58.

Negash, T. and K. Tronvoll, 2001, *Brothers At War: Making Sense Of The Eritrean-Ethiopian War*. Ohio: Ohio University Press.

Negash, T., 1997, *Eritrea and Ethiopia: The Federal Experience*. Uppsala: The Nordic Africa Institute.

Ngoga, P., 1998, "Uganda: The National Resistance Army", in Clapham, C. (ed.), *African*

Guerrilla. Oxford: James Currey, pp. 91–106.

Nugent, P. and A.I. Asiwaju, 1996, *African Boundaries: Barriers, Conduits and Opportunities*. London: Pinter.

Nyaba, P.A. and P. Otim, 2001, *Conflicts in Pastoral Areas along Borders: The Kenya, Uganda, and Sudan*. CEWARN Consultancy Report. London: FEWAR.

Nyang'oro, J E., 1999, "Civil Society, Democratization and State Building in Kenya and Tanzania", in Mengisteab, K. and C. Daddieh (eds), *State Building and Democratization in Africa*. Westpoint: Praeger, pp. 183–99.

Onyiego, M., 2010, "Analysts Say Eritrea Is Not Supporting al-Shebab," VOANews.com, 21 July.

Osamba, J.O., 2000, "The Sociology of Insecurity," *African Journal of Conflict Resolution*1(2).

Ottaway, M., 1999a, "Nation Building and State Disintegration", in Mengisteab, K. and C. Daddieh (eds), *State Building and Democratization in Africa*. Westpoint: Praeger, pp. 84–97.

Pan-African African Parliament: African Union, http://www.africa-union.org/rule_prot/protocol-panafricanparliament.pdf.

Patrick, E., 2005, "Intent to Destroy: The Genocidal Impact of Forced Migration in Darfur, Sudan", *Journal of Refugee Studies* 18(4):410–29.

Plaut, M., 2005, "The Eritrea Opposition Moves towards Unity", *Review of African Political Economy* 32(106):638–43.

Poluha, E., 1998, "Ethnicity and Democracy: A Viable Alliance?", in Salih, M.A.M. and J. Markakis (eds), *Ethnicity and the State in Eastern Africa*. Uppsala: Scandinavian Institute of African Studies.

Pool, D., 2001, *From Guerrillas to Government: The Eritrean People's Liberation Front*. Oxford: James Currey.

Potekhin, I.I., 1963, "Land Relations in African Countries", *Journal of Modern African Studies* 1(1):39–59 (March).

Pruine, G., 2007, *Darfur: The Ambiguous Genocide*, Revised and Updated Edition. Ithaca: Cornell University Press.

Quam, M.D., 1996, "Creating Peace in an Armed Society: Karamoja, Uganda", *African Studies Quarterly* 1(1):15.

Qugnivet, N., 2006, "The Report of the International Commission of Inquiry on Darfur: The Question of Genocide", *Human Rights Review* 7(4), (July):38–68.

Reid, R., 2001, "The Challenge of the Past: The Quest for Historical Legitimacy in Independent Eritrea", *History in Africa* 28:239–72.

—, 2003, "Old Problems in New Conflicts: Some Observations on Eritrea and its Relation with Tigray, from Liberation Struggle to Inter-State War", *Africa* 73(3).

Rothchild, D., 2001, "The US Foreign Policy Trajectory on Africa", *SAIS Review* XXI(1):179–211(Winter-Spring).

Rotberg, R. and I. Battling (eds), 2005, *Terrorism in the Horn of Africa*. Washington DC: Brookings Institution Press.

Sachs, J.D. and A.M. Warner, 2001, "The Curse of Natural Resources", *European Economic Review* 45(4–6):827–38.

Salehyan, I., 2008, "From Climate Change to Conflict? No Consensus Yet", *Journal of Peace Research* 45(3):315–26.

Salih, M.M.A., 1999, "Other Identities: The Politics of Sudanese Discursive Narratives", *Identities: The Journal of Global Culture and Power* 5(1):1–27.

—, 2003, *African Political Parties: Evolution, Institutionalization and Governance.* London: Pluto Press.

Samatar, A.I. and W. Machaka, 2006, "Conflict and Peace in the Horn of Africa: A Regional Approach", in *In Quest for a Culture of Peace in the IGAD Region*. Nairobi: Heinrich Boll Foundation: 26–55.

Samatar, A.I. and A.I. Samatar, 2005, "Transition and Leadership: An Editorial", *Bidhaan: An International Journal of Somali Studies,* 5.

Samatar, S., 2002, "Unhappy Masses and the Challenge of Political Islam in the Horn of Africa", *Horn of Africa* 20:1–10.

Sanders, E., 2009, "Changing Climate, changing Lives – Fleeing Drought in the Horn of Africa", *The Los Angeles Times* (25 October).

Scherrer, C.P. (ed.), n.d., "Horn of Africa: The Authentic Voice of Ethno-nationalists, Insurgents and the Democratic Opposition", Vol. 1; "Ethiopia versus Oromia: The Empire Strikes Back", Vol. 2; *Ethiopia, Eritrea and Sudan between Change and Civil War*. Moers: Institut zur Forderung der Ethnizitatsforschung und Konfliktbearbeitung (IFEK/IRECOR).

Schlee, G., 2003, "Redrawing the Map of the Horn: The Politics of Difference", Africa/International African Institute 73(3):343–68.

Shay, S., 2005, *Red Sea Terror Triangle: Sudan, Somalia, Yemen and Islamic Terror.* London: Transaction Publishers.

Sorbo, G.M. and S. Pausewang (eds), 2004, *Prospects for Peace, Security and Human Rights in Africa's Horn*. Bergen: Fagbokforlaget.

Speech by the Eritrean Permanent Mission to UN Security Council, 24 October 2008.

Swain, A., 1997, "Ethiopia, the Sudan, and Egypt: the Nile River Dispute", *Journal of Modern African Studies* 35(4):675–94.

Tadesse, M. and J. Young, 2003, "TPLF: Reform or decline?" *Review of African Political Economy* (97):389–403.

Tekle, A., 1996, "International Relations in the Horn of Africa (1991–96)", *Review of African Political Economy* 23(70):499–509.

Trevill, R., 1999, "Background Notes on the Ethiopian-Eritrean War", *Afrika Spectrum* (Fall Edition).

Twentieth Century Atlas, "Secondary Wars and Atrocities of the Twentieth Century", http://necrometrics.com/20c300k.htm (accessed September 20, 2011).

Vanhanen, T., 1999, "Domestic Ethnic Conflict and Ethnic Nepotism: A Comparative Analysis," *Journal of Peace Research*, 36(1):55–73.

Waal de, A., 2005, *Islamism and Its Enemies in the Horn of Africa*. London: Hurst.

Woodward, P., 2006, *US Foreign Policy and the Horn of Africa*. Hampshire, UK and Burlington, USA: Ashgate.

Yohannes, O., 1991, *Eritrea: A Pawn in World Politics*. Gainesville FL: University of Florida Press.

Yohannes, O., 1997, *The United States and the Horn of Africa: An Analytical Study of Pattern and Process*. Boulder CO: Westview Press.

Young, J., 2005a, "John Garang's Legacy to the Peace Process, the SPLM/A and the South", *Review of African Political Economy* 32(106):535–48.

—, 2005b, "Sudan: A Flawed Peace Process Leading to a Flawed Peace", *Review of African Political Economy* 32(103):99–113.

DISCUSSION PAPERS PUBLISHED BY THE INSTITUTE

Recent issues in the series are available electronically for download free of charge
www.nai.uu.se

1. Kenneth Hermele and Bertil Odén, *Sanctions and Dilemmas. Some Implications of Economic Sanctions against South Africa.* 1988. 43 pp. ISBN 91-7106-286-6

2. Elling Njål Tjønneland, *Pax Pretoriana. The Fall of Apartheid and the Politics of Regional Destabilisation.* 1989. 31 pp. ISBN 91-7106-292-0

3. Hans Gustafsson, Bertil Odén and Andreas Tegen, *South African Minerals. An Analysis of Western Dependence.* 1990. 47 pp. ISBN 91-7106-307-2

4. Bertil Egerö, *South African Bantustans. From Dumping Grounds to Battlefronts.* 1991. 46 pp. ISBN 91-7106-315-3

5. Carlos Lopes, *Enough is Enough! For an Alternative Diagnosis of the African Crisis.* 1994. 38 pp. ISBN 91-7106-347-1

6. Annika Dahlberg, *Contesting Views and Changing Paradigms.* 1994. 59 pp. ISBN 91-7106-357-9

7. Bertil Odén, *Southern African Futures. Critical Factors for Regional Development in Southern Africa.* 1996. 35 pp. ISBN 91-7106-392-7

8. Colin Leys and Mahmood Mamdani, *Crisis and Reconstruction – African Perspectives.* 1997. 26 pp. ISBN 91-7106-417-6

9. Gudrun Dahl, *Responsibility and Partnership in Swedish Aid Discourse.* 2001. 30 pp. ISBN 91-7106-473-7

10. Henning Melber and Christopher Saunders, *Transition in Southern Africa – Comparative Aspects.* 2001. 28 pp. ISBN 91-7106-480-X

11. *Regionalism and Regional Integration in Africa.* 2001. 74 pp. ISBN 91-7106-484-2

12. Souleymane Bachir Diagne, et al., *Identity and Beyond: Rethinking Africanity.* 2001. 33 pp. ISBN 91-7106-487-7

13. Georges Nzongola-Ntalaja, et al., *Africa in the New Millennium.* Edited by Raymond Suttner. 2001. 53 pp. ISBN 91-7106-488-5

14. *Zimbabwe's Presidential Elections 2002.* Edited by Henning Melber. 2002. 88 pp. ISBN 91-7106-490-7

15. Birgit Brock-Utne, *Language, Education and Democracy in Africa.* 2002. 47 pp. ISBN 91-7106-491-5

16. Henning Melber et al., *The New Partnership for Africa's development (NEPAD).* 2002. 36 pp. ISBN 91-7106-492-3

17. Juma Okuku, *Ethnicity, State Power and the Democratisation Process in Uganda.* 2002. 42 pp. ISBN 91-7106-493-1

18. Yul Derek Davids, et al., *Measuring Democracy and Human Rights in Southern Africa.* Compiled by Henning Melber. 2002. 50 pp. ISBN 91-7106-497-4

19. Michael Neocosmos, Raymond Suttner and Ian Taylor, *Political Cultures in Democratic South Africa.* Compiled by Henning Melber. 2002. 52 pp. ISBN 91-7106-498-2

20. Martin Legassick, *Armed Struggle and Democracy. The Case of South Africa.* 2002. 53 pp. ISBN 91-7106-504-0

21. Reinhart Kössler, Henning Melber and Per Strand, *Development from Below. A Namibian Case Study.* 2003. 32 pp. ISBN 91-7106-507-5

22. Fred Hendricks, *Fault-Lines in South African Democracy. Continuing Crises of Inequality and Injustice.* 2003. 32 pp. ISBN 91-7106-508-3

23. Kenneth Good, *Bushmen and Diamonds. (Un) Civil Society in Botswana.* 2003. 39 pp. ISBN 91-7106-520-2

24. Robert Kappel, Andreas Mehler, Henning Melber and Anders Danielson, *Structural Stability in an African Context.* 2003. 55 pp. ISBN 91-7106-521-0

25. Patrick Bond, *South Africa and Global Apartheid. Continental and International Policies and Politics.* 2004. 45 pp. ISBN 91-7106-523-7

26. Bonnie Campbell (ed.), *Regulating Mining in Africa. For whose benefit?* 2004. 89 pp. ISBN 91-7106-527-X

27. Suzanne Dansereau and Mario Zamponi, *Zimbabwe – The Political Economy of Decline.* Compiled by Henning Melber. 2005. 43 pp. ISBN 91-7106-541-5

28. Lars Buur and Helene Maria Kyed, *State Recog-nition of Traditional Authority in Mozambique. The nexus of Community Representation and State Assist-ance.* 2005. 30 pp. ISBN 91-7106-547-4

29. Hans Eriksson and Björn Hagströmer, *Chad – Towards Democratisation or Petro-Dictatorship?* 2005. 82 pp.ISBN 91-7106-549-

30. Mai Palmberg and Ranka Primorac (eds), *Skinning the Skunk – Facing Zimbabwean Futures.* 2005. 40 pp. ISBN 91-7106-552-0

31. Michael Brüntrup, Henning Melber and Ian Taylor, *Africa, Regional Cooperation and the World Market – Socio-Economic Strategies in Times of Global Trade Regimes.* Com-piled by Henning Melber. 2006. 70 pp. ISBN 91-7106-559-8

32. Fibian Kavulani Lukalo, *Extended Handshake or Wrestling Match? – Youth and Urban Culture Celebrating Politics in Kenya.* 2006.58 pp. ISBN 91-7106-567-9

33. Tekeste Negash, *Education in Ethiopia: From Crisis to the Brink of Collapse.* 2006. 55 pp. ISBN 91-7106-576-8

34. Fredrik Söderbaum and Ian Taylor (eds) *Micro-Regionalism in West Africa. Evidence from Two Case Studies.* 2006. 32 pp. ISBN 91-7106-584-9

35. Henning Melber (ed.), *On Africa – Scholars and African Studies.* 2006. 68 pp. ISBN 978-91-7106-585-8

36. Amadu Sesay, *Does One Size Fit All? The Sierra Leone Truth and Reconciliation Commission Revisited.* 2007. 56 pp. ISBN 978-91-7106-586-5

37. Karolina Hulterström, Amin Y. Kamete and Henning Melber, *Political Opposition in African Countries – The Case of Kenya, Namibia, Zambia and Zimbabwe.* 2007. 86 pp. ISBN 978-7106-587-2

38. Henning Melber (ed.), *Governance and State Delivery in Southern Africa. Examples from Botswana, Namibia and Zimbabwe.* 2007. 65 pp. ISBN 978-91-7106-587-2

39. Cyril Obi (ed.), *Perspectives on Côte d'Ivoire: Between Political Breakdown and Post-Conflict Peace.* 2007. 66 pp. ISBN 978-91-7106-606-6

40. Anna Chitando, *Imagining a Peaceful Society. A Vision of Children's Literature in a Post-Conflict Zimbabwe.* 2008. 26 pp. ISBN 978-91-7106-623-7

41. Olawale Ismail, *The Dynamics of Post-Conflict Reconstruction and Peace Building in West Africa. Between Change and Stability.* 2009.52 pp. ISBN 978-91-7106-637-4

42. Ron Sandrey and Hannah Edinger, *Examining the South Africa–China Agricultural Relationship.* 2009. 58 pp. ISBN 978-91-7106-643-5

43. Xuan Gao, *The Proliferation of Anti-Dumping and Poor Governance in Emerging Economies.* 2009. 41 pp. ISBN 978-91-7106-644-2

44. Lawal Mohammed Marafa, *Africa's Business and Development Relationship with China. Seeking Moral and Capital Values of the Last Economic Frontier.* 2009. xx pp. ISBN 978-91-7106-645-9

45. Mwangi wa Githinji, *Is That a Dragon or an Elephant on Your Ladder? The Potential Impact of China and India on Export Led Growth in African Countries.* 2009. 40 pp. ISBN 978-91-7106-646-6

46. Jo-Ansie van Wyk, *Cadres, Capitalists, Elites and Coalitions. The ANC, Business and Development in South Africa.* 2009. 61 pp. ISBN 978-91-7106-656-5

47. Elias Courson, *Movement for the Emancipation of the Niger Delta (MEND). Political Marginalization, Repression and Petro-Insurgency in the Niger Delta.*2009. 30 pp. ISBN 978-91-7106-657-2

48. Babatunde Ahonsi, *Gender Violence and HIV/AIDS in Post-Conflict West Africa. Issues and Responses.* 2010. 38 pp. ISBN 978-91-7106-665-7

49. Usman Tar and Abba Gana Shettima, *Endangered Democracy? The Struggle over Secularism and its Implications for Politics and Democracy in Nigeria.* 2010. 21 pp. ISBN 978-91-7106-666-4

50. Garth Andrew Myers, *Seven Themes in African Urban Dynamics.*2010. 28 pp. ISBN 978-91-7106-677-0

51. Abdoumaliq Simone, *The Social Infrastructures of City Life in Contemporary Africa.* 2010. 33 pp. ISBN 978-91-7106-678-7

52. Li Anshan, *Chinese Medical Cooperation in Africa. With Special Emphasis on the Medical Teams and Anti-Malaria Campaign.* 2011. 24 pp. ISBN 978-91-7106-683-1

53. Folashade Hunsu, *Zangbeto: Navigating the Spaces Between Oral art, Communal Security And Conflict Mediation in Badagry, Nigeria.* 2011. 27 pp. ISBN 978-91-7106-688-6

54. Jeremiah O. Arowosegbe, *Reflections on the Challenge of Reconstructing Post-Conflict States in West Africa: Insights from Claude Ake's Political Writings.*
2011. 40 pp. ISBN 978-91-7106-689-3

55. Bertil Odén, *The Africa Policies of Nordic Countries and the Erosion of the Nordic Aid Model: A comparative study.*
2011. 66 pp. ISBN 978-91-7106-691-6

56. Angela Meyer, *Peace and Security Cooperation in Central Africa: Developments, Challenges and Prospects.*
2011. 47 pp ISBN 978-91-7106-693-0

57. Godwin R. Murunga, *Spontaneous or Premeditated? Post-Election Violence in Kenya.*
2011. 58 pp. ISBN 978-91-7106-694-7

58. David Sebudubudu & Patrick Molutsi, *The Elite as a Critical Factor in National Development: The Case of Botswana.*
2011. 48 pp. ISBN 978-91-7106-695-4

59. Sabelo J. Ndlovu-Gatsheni, *The Zimbabwean Nation-State Project. A Historical Diagnosis of Identity and Power-Based Conflicts in a Postcolonial State.*
2011. 97 pp. ISBN 978-91-7106-696-1

60. Jide Okeke, *Why Humanitarian Aid in Darfur is not a Practice of the 'Responsibility to Protect'.*
2011. 45 pp. ISBN 978-91-7106-697-8

61. Florence Odora Adong, *Recovery and Development Politics. Options for Sustainable Peacebuilding in Northern Uganda.*
2011, 72 pp. ISBN 978-91-7106-698-5

62. Osita A. Agbu, *Ethnicity and Democratisation in Africa. Challenges for Politics and Development.*
2011, 30 pp. ISBN 978-91-7106-699-2

63. Cheryl Hendricks, *Gender and Security in Africa. An Overview.*
2011, 32 pp. ISBN 978-91-7106-700-5

64. Adebayo O. Olukoshi, *Democratic Governance and Accountability in Africa. In Search of a Workable Framework.*
2011, 25 pp. ISBN 978-91-7106-701-2

65. Christian Lund, *Land Rights and Citizenship in Africa.*
2011, 31 pp. ISBN 978-91-7106-705-0

66. Lars Rudebeck, *Electoral Democratisation in Post-Civil War Guinea-Bissau 1999–2008.*
2011, 31 pp. ISBN 978-91-7106-706-7

67. Kidane Mengisteab, *Critical Factors in the Horn of Africa's Raging Conflicts.*
2011, 39 pp. ISBN 978-91-7106-707-4

www.ingramcontent.com/pod-product-compliance
Lightning Source LLC
Chambersburg PA
CBHW080210300326
41934CB00039B/3438